THE TRUTH ABOUT MANIPULATORS

How to defend yourself from emotional manipulative people and take control of your life

MARGIE J. LARUE

TABLE OF CONTENT

A marriage of 30 years to a narcissistic woman

I was married to a narcissistic woman for 30 years. Everything seemed OK at first. I couldn't do anything wrong, and everything I did was perfect. This was the love-bombing phase. I mistakenly imagined that this would be my life. I had married the ideal woman. She was sweet, helpful, and loving.

Sex was plentiful and often We married, bought a house, and had a kid together. This was the love-bombing phase. My professional career took off. I received honors for my productivity, and I was given a larger office, more personnel, and larger incentives.

But it seemed like no matter how much I earned, it was never enough. I eventually got bored of the hamster wheel of employment and launched my own business. That's when everything started to go sour.

Because even though I made more money on my own than I ever did working, it was never enough. I had more time and the capacity to appreciate life.

That, however, was not acceptable to my wife. If I had more time, I could make more money, and she could have more stuff.

I was now indolent and didn't have a genuine job because I didn't get paid by anyone else. This started the devaluation period. I was constantly criticized for not doing enough or doing incorrectly

Sex became less frequent. I initially blamed everything on having children, but I ultimately began to internalize the criticism. I increased my efforts. My reply was merely more criticism and scorn. I developed depression and stopped seeing friends and relatives.

I gradually assumed more and more home responsibilities. I cooked and cleaned, did laundry, and took care of the yard and house. It didn't matter. I was still ridiculed. She had begun working and was now earning more than $80,000 per year. But still I paid all of the bills.

She began working more and more. When the weekend arrived, she would frequently spend time with her girlfriends, going on overnight excursions and taking vacations.

Sex became scarce, and if I mentioned how long it had been, her response was disregard and mockery. Whenever we had a disagreement, it generally ended with her telling me, "I am doing the best I can, and if you don't like it, I am leaving!"

This always resulted in my slinking away, thinking about what a monster I must be for expecting the lady I loved, who professed to love me, to want to be with me as well. I'd eventually apologize, she'd toss me a bone, and then quickly return to whatever had sparked the discussion in the first place.

Finally, after a 30-year marriage, I was just dumped with no explanation. By the end of it all, I had no idea who I was or what I wanted out of life.

I was heartbroken when I discovered she had been cheating. It took me years to get back to normal. Even now, eight years later, I find myself doubting myself and my aspirations.

But things are looking up. I no longer have a parasite eating me dry. I have more money, more savings, no debt, and a stronger connection with my children, their wives, and their children than I would have had if I had remained married.

INTRODUCTION

Narcissists manipulate because their entire being is a lie! Because their home situation as young kids were not healthy, they learned to become NPD between the ages of 2 and 7. Narcissism is a learned behavior.

In general, the kid has a parent or caretaker who is selfish, self-centered, emotionally, physically, or sexually abusive, domineering, passive-aggressive, critical, and incapable of loving and guiding them as they develop their personality.

The parenting style might be abusive; abandonment due to substance misuse, work, or moving on in life and leaving the kid behind; controlling behaviors; and authoritarian parenting methods. Another aspect is that parents have a propensity for putting their young child on a pedestal or being a child-centered household.

All of these parental behaviors may lead a young child to feel mistreated, abandoned, fearful, uncertain, with poor self-esteem, invalidated, worthless, with lots of insecurities, and scared—you name it—and it impacts and scars them for life!

They believe no one in their life's cares about them, so they withdraw within themselves and believe it is "me against the world." They learn to fend for themselves. They learn how to meet their wants by lying, cheating, and influencing others through gaslighting and projections.

Then, as young adults, they learned how to put on the "Mask of Perfection" in public so that they would be accepted and able to live the life they desired.

Behind that mask lies a "little kid" (an emotionally stunted adult) who feels they must do all possible to defend this mask at all costs! As a result, an NPD has complete control over everyone and everything around them.

The price you pay for being the main person in your life is confusion, fog-like feelings, unhappiness, sadness to the core of your being, isolation from family and friends, loneliness, and a total lack of love.

They are incapable of loving anyone, including their children, because they only love and care about themselves. You must comprehend that kids are incapable of understanding or expressing love in a healthy adult manner.

They are incapable of caring about anybody or their sentiments. They simply care about themselves, and their feelings are what matters. They can't do it. It is completely unfamiliar to them.

They are, nevertheless, capable of "love bombing" you early in the relationship. They are incredibly attentive and pleasant, purchase costly gifts, eat at excellent restaurants, and look lovely in every manner, but it is all a sham! ruse to get you into their intricate network of lies, deception, and cruelty! They should come with a warning notice!

Knowing or sparing a manipulator Manipulative people have one thing in common: they are really infantile.
These are the folks who never learned to set limits or respect others' boundaries. These are the individuals who believe that if they push and push their partners or anybody else, they know, they will finally get their way, and the others around them will cave in.

These are people who have probably witnessed a dynamic, such as growing up knowing their parents, where the mother is a bit manipulative, or, to put it another way, narcissistic.

while the father is a simpleton who constantly wants the mother to have her way, such as controlling the outcome of the issue and finally receiving what they want from someone.

Manipulators are exceedingly insecure, with fragile egos. You never say no to them; if you do, you open a gash in their egos.

A manipulative person has never learned to accept and deal with rejection. They are highly competitive in life; life is a game to them. It doesn't matter who is winning, who is losing, or who has the power.

These are not the types of individuals who will sit down and objectively consider what is fair or compromise able with you. NO! They just care about winning and getting what they want when they want it.

They are the ones that, when they ask you a question, want a quick response and will not allow you a second to consider what you want and how you feel.

They simply want you to contribute and respond as soon as possible. When you advise a manipulative person to give you time, they will not like it and will not stop until you respond.

The problem is that these are individuals who know you well; they know your worries, they know where your scars are, and they will use whatever techniques they can to obtain what they want from you.

So, they will use your variability against you to control the circumstances and the outcome, which is to acquire what they want from you. When all else fails and they still don't get what they want from you.

Here is where it **really?** Comes to play. Then the abusive behavior begins, with the bullying, threatening, and name-calling of you being selfish and me doing everything for you but you never being there for me.

They use all of these varied strategies to make you doubt yourself, to make you believe that your feelings about them are incorrect, and that you should give them what they want because they deserve it (entitlement is also present in a manipulative person).

It doesn't matter how you feel or what you want; this is what they want, and they believe they deserve to receive everything they want at any time.

And if you do not provide them, you will face consequences These are the individuals who will draw easy people like you into their lives since people like you don't always have a strong sense of self-worth or a firm foundation of self-worth.

They know you're just easygoing and will typically give people anything they want without really thinking about it in any situation. So, when you begin to love yourself, you prioritize yourself; you are always linked to how you feel and what you desire.

Even if you don't know, you should inform the individual if you are unsure what to say.

CHAPTER ONE

How do manipulators discard their partners?

A narcissist will reject you in the most brutal way conceivable. It will hit you like a hard rock out of left field. You will emerge from it perplexed, befuddled, and disoriented, not understanding how the person who professed to adore every aspect of you now finds you repulsive.

You don't understand how, after spending so much time together and maintaining in touch, you've been blocked, ostracized, cut off, and demeaned. You can't believe how harsh they are to you when all you did was be kind to them. You move from being the focus of their attention to them wanting nothing to do with you.

You will be promptly demoted from their supply chain once they have grown tired of you, as they do with every single individual they trap in their toxic web. They no longer care to keep you around once they have used up all of the excellent things you have done for them.

You were once their favorite and number one option, but they will push you to the curb with a new person fully groomed to take your place. This individual is now taking up all of their free time, getting all of their full attention, and love-bombing.

They're saying all the beautiful things to them that you used to say to them. While they are eliminating you from their lives, they are praising this new person for how important they are. They have discovered someone who they believe is "better" than what you have supplied them.

Manipulators need variety and do not want to settle down or attend to the demands of one person for the rest of their lives. That is ridiculous to them. They enjoy the notion of people being devoted to them, but this will never be reciprocated.

They want to be allowed to sleep with anybody they want without hesitation, and they want you to put up with it or else you will be flung away in an instant.

They want to be allowed to flirt with your neighbors, strangers, friends, relatives, coworkers, or any random person they met online or at a club, and they want you to look the other way and accept it, or else you are insane, jealous, insecure, and controlling.

They want to be able to utilize their social media platforms to connect with other people and couldn't care less about your thoughts about it. They want to be able to spend all of their money on drinking and drugs, partying, the sex industry, gambling, or anything else other than taking care of duties.

Then they will go ahead and squander all of your hard-earned money without hesitation. They will want you to bend over backward for them, surrendering your dignity, self-respect, and individuality, and nothing will ever be enough for them, no matter how hard you try.

They used to like hearing from you, but now they find everything you do or say irritating.

They'll accuse you of suffocating them, of being needy, clinging, and domineering.

They will do all of these things on purpose, and then blame you for it. You will eventually confront them because it is becoming too much for you and you feel like you are continuously walking on eggshells just to make them happy.

They will reject you if you begin to call them out on their chaotic, destructive, impulsive, irresponsible, and risky conduct. In their minds, they say, "How dare you hold me accountable for purposefully injuring you!! "You idiot, off you go." They don't want to hear how much sorrow, anguish, distress, or abuse they have caused in your life.

They don't want to hear how outraged you are because you caught them lying, cheating, or flirting with other people. They don't want to hear how they've been ignoring all of your messages and avoiding you. They want to be free to live their lives as they like, without being held accountable for the consequences of their acts.

They will also abandon you to get control of you. They do this only to see how far they can push you.

You may be having the finest time together one minute and then wake up to find that you've been blocked, they've changed their phone number, moved, quit their jobs, and vanished.

This will put you in a panic and make you feel abandoned because you developed so close to them. You spend all of your time going insane and trying to get through each day when you can barely function.

They leave you in excruciating pain while seemingly moving on with their life and slithering like manipulative snakes onto the next victim with no consideration for how they've left you to bleed out.

They will dump you, but not before they have made you feel absolutely useless, sad, alone, and devastated. Before they send you away, their purpose is to drain more supplies from you by witnessing you fall on your knees in misery, not knowing how it all came to this.

They adore watching you give up everything for them, even when they know there are others in queue wanting to do the same.

You don't comprehend how all the great memories and fantastic moments you shared have suddenly collapsed to shambles in bits while they are building them with someone else.

They dump you because they don't care about you. They truly do not. This is the most crucial point to grasp. While you may be in love with them, be loyal, faithful, and generous; they do not think the same way you do. They have no concept of commitment or what it means to compromise for another person. They think about themselves at all times and will not allow anyone to get in their way.

They might tell you that they want to spend the rest of their life with you and that they will never leave you, and the next time you turn around, they will be with someone else telling them the same things and have tossed you out of their lives faster than you can blink. They want the freedom to do anything they want, no questions asked.

They dump you because it gives them a rush to know they have authority and power over you. They like watching you beg, plead, cry, and lose yourself over them. They are spreading lies about you to their friends and anybody else who will listen about what an awful person you are.

Meanwhile, they're omitting all of the heinous things they said and did to you. When you try to connect with them, they will label you as a crazy, stalker, bothersome, jealous ex who won't leave them alone.

They do this to make you jealous of their fresh supply. They want to give the impression that they have people falling head over heels for them and that they have endless possibilities.

They will dismiss you since they do not attach themselves to others. They will utilize whoever benefits them, and whenever something more appealing comes along, you will be gone in an instant. They may disconnect you for days, weeks, months, or even years and then abruptly resurface if it suits their requirements.

They believe they can come and leave anytime they choose, no matter how much time has gone or how much harm they have inflicted. They make certain that they choose the most empathetic folks since we are the most forgiving. They will know exactly what to say and do to win you back, and it will be the same continuous cycle of abuse.

They will dump you at the worst possible time. You might be facing some severe circumstances, and they will take advantage of the situation to forsake you. They do this to demonstrate that they will not hold your hand during difficult times and will not be someone on whom you can rely.

They will consider anything you are going through to be a nuisance to them, so they will just drop you off for one of their other supplies that aren't "whining and grumbling" attack and call. They will reject you on your birthday, holidays, or any other significant event.

If you are looking forward to something, they will find a way to destroy it for you by ghosting you, giving you quiet treatment, and refusing to communicate with you.

They will also dump you to ensure that you remain obedient and docile for future use. If they cut you off as punishment for standing up for yourself and you come back around begging, they know they'll have you right in the palm of their hands when they decide to worm their way back in, since you so badly want to sort things out with them.

You are willing to ignore all that has occurred to see them again. You are prepared to give up your limits to allow a more open connection that meets their requirements since you don't want to lose them again. You're willing to try new sexual experiences only to make them happy. It's all crazy!

They treat you like a slave and will abandon you in a second, no matter how much you loved and cared for, or how long you've known them. It doesn't matter if you've been together for decades, months, or weeks; they will do whatever they want, when they want, with whoever they want, for as long as they live.

They will dump you cruelly and without remorse. They will do it unexpectedly as if they are holding a pistol to the back of your head and pulling the trigger after hearing your cries. They will come at you with full power, like a blunt trauma strike, and watch you suffer. They will stab you in the back and twist the knife even more each time you allow them to come back for more.

They aren't worth your time, tears, sympathy, effort, or love. The longer you stay with them, and the longer you wait for them to desire you again, you will lose yourself a bit more each time until you no longer recognize yourself.

That is not a life worth living. you deserve to be loved back when they give their best. Nobody should have to endure abuse, be cheated on, and be constantly insulted for the sake of one person.

We wouldn't want our friends or family to go through that, so why would we desire that for ourselves? Never believe that you aren't good enough, that you will never find someone else, or that you will never be happy. Anything is preferable to being repeatedly abused, exploited, stepped on, degraded, betrayed, and put aside like rubbish.

"The ones who are eager to leave are the ones who never planned to remain."

CHAPTER 2

TACTICS AND WHAT THEY SAY

The motive for manipulation differs depending on the abuser or manipulator, but one thing all manipulators have in common is a desire for control. Some people thrive on feeling superior to another person in order to acquire what they want from you.

So, they need something to obtain what they want, so they will employ manipulative techniques to achieve what they want. Their purpose is to dominate you and force you to do whatever they desire.

When they seek that type of domination or control over you, it just makes them feel better about themselves because it indicates that someone is genuinely listening to them or paying attention to them.

Someone who is narcissistic, an abuser, or simply generally poisonous and sick thrives on these traits. Remember that when dealing with someone who is insecure and has poor self-esteem, it may not always look that way, but it is the overarching message of all manipulators.

It makes them feel important; it makes them feel full inside because someone is not only listening to them but actually doing what they want.

Manipulation strategies are used by the narcissist to gain the victim's respect.

Love Bombing-They will elevate the victim to a pedestal, making him feel unique, gaining his love, trust, dedication, respect, value, and admiration, leaving the victim defenseless to their charm and affection.

Giving the victim everything, they want and need to hear, the victim will let down his guard and believe he has discovered his true match. He has no clue what will happen next, and he won't be prepared for it.

Mirroring highly deceptive methods utilized by the Narcissists to secure their Supply. They will absorb your personality features, share your hobbies, and dress in your manner.

They, and the victim will be astonished by the things you have in common and how angelic-caring-lovely this catch can be while she is still unmarried and feels like the luckiest person in the world.

Essentially, the Narcissist is winning the victim's confidence while connecting him to their love and care. This allows the Narcissist to further influence you with the strategies I'll discuss next, leaving the victim even more enslaved to the cycle of abuse.

Manipulation strategies are used after they have gained the victim's love and have begun to depreciate.

Once they have gained the victim's affection, trust, value, respect, dedication, and admiration, they are likely to get bored since they cannot love anybody, even themselves, or empathize with people.

They see people as simply character extensions or things. The depreciation occurs for two reasons:

1. They just become bored with you because they seek drama and excitement and you supply them with boredom with your steadiness and sentiments.

2. You saw through that mask or veneer and began voicing your viewpoint while calling them out on their conduct; they now perceive you as a threat to their safety.

Once the devaluation begins, there is no turning back; it is all about the manipulation of games to keep the source of supply in line.

The victim's devaluation is the most eye-opening experience in life; the victim begins to see that the person they believed they were in love with never existed; it was an act or illusion produced by the Con Artist (The NPD).

You must learn and find the inner strength to move forward; you must accept the reality that you were manipulated and lied to by the Con Artist; you will have severe withdrawal symptoms as a result of the trauma bond and abuse by the abuser; you will hold on to hope when there is none, to begin with; and you must fight constantly with their mindset until you go full No Contact and break free from this abusive drug.

When the NPD becomes bored with the victim and begins to look for new sources while degrading their victim, their most powerful weapon is silence.
Silent treatment is a passive-aggressive strategy employed by emotional abusers to avoid accountability for their acts, further dominate the victim, leave the victim confused, and emotionally destroy them.

The NPD will offer you his/her quiet to neutralize any attempts by you to call them out on their conduct and start over.

This occurs when the NPD has obtained your affection or is looking for fresh resources. This might happen gradually or all at once, depending on the abuser. Gradually, their silence will increase as a kind of punishment for being called out on their acts.

Diversion, also known as Stone Walling, occurs when you repeatedly call them out on their activities and they deny everything. They will become enraged and begin to punish you not only with their silence but also with the Emotional Withhold, which is anything that does not feel good for you during the Love Bombing phase.

They will withhold emotions and show no affection at all. You will drive yourself insane if you ask them what happened, why it happened, and what you did. They will never provide any answers, just neutral dull answers, while they enjoy the abuse to the fullest.

When you inquire if they still feel the same way they did, they will say they don't know, thus leaving you hanging and providing no answers. When you ask them what occurred, they will say nothing or I don't know.

When you bring up the subject of affection, they will change the subject to something else, essentially putting a stone wall between you and getting no answers.

The more you seek closure or answers, the less they will give it to you, because that gives them power and makes them feel important with the control, they have over you. You will walk away from the conversation more perplexed and without solutions.

Gaslighting, also known as crazy-making, is one of their favorite weapons for driving the victim insane, leaving them defenseless and emotionally drained.

They will slap you today and tell you they didn't do it tomorrow and act like nothing happened, because deep down inside they know how emotionally connected you are to them and you won't leave no matter what because they sniffed your empathic traits while they were testing you on the love bombing phase and trying to see how far they could walk away while crossing your boundaries.

You will begin to doubt your sanity and vision since, from this point forward, everything is dependent on their validation and how they view you as a character because they have connected you to their love and affection.

Projection, also known as blame shifting, occurs when you confront them about their actions. They will play the victim card, posing as the innocent one, and shift the blame to you.

They will tell you that you are insane that they did not do these things, and that you need to stop overthinking because you will drive yourself insane.

You will find things never said pardoned, and they will be the ones to forgive you.

Discard: On the abuser's side, they prefer to keep the victims puzzled for a future return. Most victims will quit because they have had enough of the abuse.

Most of the time, lengthy Silent Treatments are mistaken for discards. It is more likely to occur if the victim is perceived as a threat to their safety or mask since they live to maintain that mask or facade.

Hoovering-The Narcissist's potential comeback to drag you back into the game. They will re-emerge as if nothing occurred and attempt to take up where they left off.

They will begin to idealize again, telling you how much they missed you, how they made a mistake, how much you mean to them, and how dumb they have been, and they will cry, plead, and cling to you so you will accept them back since they lack a face and morality.

This is an NPD performance. It might happen for a variety of reasons, including a lack of new supplies or a desire to test the waters to see whether they have an impact on your life. Any reply from you would provide them with fuel or supplies.

They may have come looking for a connection or a fast fix to make you react. Most of the time, if they come for a fast fix, they will try to irritate you so you may respond in either a good or bad way, and then they will resume their quiet treatment.

Smear tactics stalking- When toxic people can't control how you perceive yourself, they try controlling how others view you; they play the martyr while you're labeled the poisonous one. A smear campaign is a preemptive strike to ruin your reputation and trash your name so that you don't have a support network to fall back on if you decide to detach and sever connections with this poisonous individual.

They may even pursue and harass you or others you know to ostensibly "reveal" the truth about you; this exposure serves to conceal their abusive behavior while projecting it onto you.

Some smear campaigns can even be used to put two persons or organizations against each other. A victim in an abusive relationship with a narcissist frequently has no idea what is being said about them throughout the relationship, but they ultimately find out the lies shortly after they've been dumped.

Toxic people will gossip behind your back (and in front of your face), slander you to your loved ones or their loved ones, fabricate stories that portray you as the aggressor while they play the victim, and claim that you engaged in the same behaviors that they are afraid you will accuse them of engaging in.

They will also assault you systematically, discreetly, and purposefully so that they can exploit your emotions to claim that they are the so-called "victims" of your abuse.

The easiest method to deal with a smear campaign is to be careful of your responses and stick to the truth.

This is especially important in high-conflict divorces with narcissists who may exploit your reactions to their provocations against you.

Document any instances of harassment, cyberbullying, or stalking, and always communicate with your narcissist through a lawyer whenever feasible.

If you believe the stalking and harassment are out of hand, you may choose to pursue legal action; finding a lawyer who is well-versed in Narcissistic Personality Disorder is critical in your scenario. When the narcissist's phony mask begins to fall, your character and integrity will speak for themselves.

Triangulation is the act of incorporating another person's viewpoint, perspective, or potential danger into the dynamic of an engagement.

Triangulation, which is frequently used to justify the toxic person's abuse while discrediting the victim's reactions to abuse, may also be used to create love triangles that leave you feeling disoriented and insecure.

Malignant manipulator like triangulating their significant other with strangers, coworkers, ex-partners, friends, and even family members to instill envy and insecurity in you. They also utilize the views of others to justify their point of view.

This is a diversionary approach designed to divert your attention away from their abusive behavior and negative negative nature of them as desirable, sought-after people.
It also makes you doubt yourself - if Mary agreed with Tom, doesn't it indicate you're wrong?

The truth is that narcissists like "reporting back" falsehoods about you that others say about you, but in reality, they are the ones ruining you.

Recognize that whatever the narcissist is triangulating with is also being triangulated by your connection with the narcissist.

This one individual is effectively playing everyone. Reverse "triangulate" the narcissist by receiving support from a third person who is not under the narcissist's control - and also by seeking your approval.

CHAPTER 3

Can a narcissist manipulate people against you?

It's a must and part of the narcissist playbook. Unfortunately, there are always some who are willing to believe the worst. The good news is that they are not a major setback.

Anyone who knows you well is unlikely to approve of your choice of mate. The manipulator has most likely shown your friends, family, and others what lies behind the mask. The goal is to drive away your support system, and they have no bounds. They like scaring people away and are generally successful.

My best friend was being watched by her narc husband. He cloned her phone, hacked her Facebook, and sent horrible messages to her friends and family while posing as her. Needless to say, his family was not thrilled, and he was already barred from entering their houses or lives.

He used the same trick on the cops when he tried to drive her off the road, stating he was concerned she was driving "drunk" and was attempting to stop her.

He succeeded once more in holding her hostage and refused to let her leave - claiming he took her vehicle keys away to prevent her from driving while drunk.

The most difficult aspect of manipulators is getting cops involved. Asses don't realize it's 2023, not 1825, and a call from an abused drug victim isn't "domestic" - it's criminal! It took me 11 months to persuade police that I was not a willful participant, but rather a victim.

My acquaintance was ultimately able to get away with wearing only the clothing on her back, and he spent a year wearing an ankle bracelet. My ex has been free for almost 12 weeks since 2022.

Only if the manipulators are a brother, parent, or stepparent is there an exemption. Unfortunately, few others anticipate a parent or family member to manipulate their own - this is incorrect.

They are the hardest to protect against, therefore you will always be at risk until you are ready to walk away. The good news is that when you vanish, they simply move on to another victim, so most people eventually figure it out.

Narcissists, at least in part, manipulate people to feel...

- **Anchored**

- **Stable**

- **Grounded**

The manipulators Proclivity to Manipulate stems from past experiences.

When the narcissist manipulates others, he is doing to his loved ones what was done to him or by his inconsistent cares. Just like his incompetent and/or mean-spirited cares acted towards the narcissist, he replicates the same behaviors with his significant others.

The Narcissists Need to Test, Test, and Test Some More
When viewing the world via a narcissistic lens, narcissists feel compelled to constantly test their SOs.

The narcissist desires to constantly discern...

•How much the narcissist is adored by the SO

•How much is the SO willing to put up with before abandoning the narcissist?

•whether the SO is perhaps duping or misleading the narcissist

The Narcissist Child Received Mixed Messages

Because they failed to fulfill their parenting responsibilities, the narcissist's caregiver(s) sent contradictory signals to their developing children:

•Their parents were nasty at times and affectionate at others.

•Sometimes they were attentive, but other times they treated the youngster as if she didn't exist.

•At times, they were responsible and kind; at others, they were neglectful or violent.

Insidious Critical Inner Voice

Given the circumstances, it is not unexpected that their inconsistently dysfunctional parenting approach led to their children having a highly critical inner voice.

A scathing internal debate...

•fears of abandonment

•fears of engulfment

•issues of trust

•problems with likability

•qualification problems

•an inability to be alone at times/feeling too restricted and "not free" at others.

The Narcissist Abuses His or Her Significant Others in the Same Way That the Narcissist Was Abused When the narcissistic child grows into an adult, he will commit the same crimes on his SO that his abusive cares did on him.

The narcissist appears to be retaliating or punishing his or her parents vicariously through the SO.

Push-Pull Behavior Is an Example of Past Learned Maladaptive Behavior Revisited on The Narcissist's Significant Others.

The narcissists SO has no way of knowing he or she has been assigned the duty of surrogate career.

The SO is also ignorant that if the narcissist feels sufficiently attached to him, he will be able to shed the mask/let down his guard and simply be himself, which will not bode well for the SO.

Adult narcissists, I believe, are vicariously retaliating against their abusive cares by lashing out at those who have the unfortunate distinction of being cares by proxy — their significant others.

The narcissist's iron wall of inappropriate ways of coping defenses appears to have been implanted into "the narcissist's hard drive" as a youngster.

To link the SO to the narcissist, I believe the narcissist employs manipulative methods such as push-pull behaviors.

Furthermore, the push-pull manipulation acts as a litmus test for the narcissist to determine the SO's level of commitment.

Finally, regardless of the narcissist's chosen defense, such as push-pull techniques, projection, projective identification, and so on...All of these manipulative behaviors are maladaptive ways for the narcissist to feel protected.

Unfortunately, in a narcissistic society, the narcissist has a drive to manipulate his SOs to have POWER and CONTROL over them.

CHAPTER4

Why does narcissistic manipulation occur?

Depending on what occurred to the narcissist as a child and how much power it had over them, they formed habits and different methods to adapt and deal with it. They discovered what they could control, even the smallest of details.

The idea was that someone would not let me say what I was thinking, would leave me alone when I was afraid, would violate me in the dark, would only allow me to eat at a certain time even though I was very hungry earlier, would leave me with someone who verbally or physically abused me, would force me to wear clothes I despised because kids teased me, would never let me sleep with my door open, and so on.

A sense of absolute powerlessness as a youngster, with no control over anything, made them feel as if they didn't matter.

As time passes, coping strategies become habits, habits get embedded and become a way of life, and whatever works for them offers them control, and control gives them power, so they try to perfect them.

They learn to read people to determine what talents to use to manipulate them into getting what they desire. This repeatedly restores the control they lacked as children. They never got over or overcame their feelings of worthlessness, so when they are critiqued or criticized, they blame,

Gaslight, lie, divert, deflect, take no responsibility, and attempt to make it all about you. They will not confess they were wrong, they are incredibly passive-hostile, and they will never apologize since most of them believe that "nothing in this world is more terrible than what happened to you," they cannot keep emphasizing empathy they continue to refine their talents as they encounter new people with diverse personality features throughout their lives. They have unlimited tolerance; they had to acquire patience to bear their infancy.

Never underestimate one, and never try to fix them since they will take it as a hostile attempt to control them. After all, the individuals who made them feel unimportant were pleasant to them, bought them presents, and even said, "I love you."

They don't need whatever you have to offer since their existence revolves around them. Some may have pets and appear to care about them since the pets cannot see or judge them, they manage the pets, and they become everything to the pets, but if that pet requires medical attention, is in agony, or otherwise requires assistance, they will not receive assistance because there is no empathy.

Don't ever assume you can offer them enough love to change them since they have no concept of what it's like to receive it because it appears like control and something to take away their power, and they're still worthless to themselves. So, to answer your question, who would dare to fall in love with someone like this?

They are aware of this, so if you have what they desire, the observation and manipulation begin. Unless you pay attention to the red signs and cut all relationships, they will have the grip of a pit bull, the patience of Job, and will eat, devour, and abandon you.

Most people have four characteristics that make them look weak and foolish to manipulators, and they are

Love, truth, trusts enlightened self-interest
Narcissists lack all four, which explains their perplexing talents. The four traits place internal limitations on outward behavior, restricting and preventing us from performing numerous things, thereby reducing our potential to get advantages through unscrupulous methods.

I can see the narcissist's point of view that these characteristics make us weak since they limit our capacity to control and get an edge over others. On an equal playing field, a narcissist with the same ability is likely to get ahead of others.

For example, if you love someone, you are afraid to damage them; yet, because the narcissist does not love anyone, they have no prohibitions against injuring anyone. Love for the narcissist is a stepping stone or an open door to benefits and rewards with no following burden when something even better comes along.

If you lie, you know you're lying, which makes your lies unconvincing because your body will betray you, but for narcissists, lies are truth, they can even convince their bodies, they believe their lies, which makes them excellent liars since they lie to themselves. You cannot.

You don't want to betray people's confidence in you, and you trust them not to betray your trust in them. The narcissist sees trust as an opening; they trust no one and do not want to trust anybody, but they know they cannot let anyone know this, so they learn which masks get the greatest trust and then intend to abuse that trust eventually.

They want others to trust them and provide opportunities for them, yet they distrust everyone and provide no opportunities.

In the end, this does not work out; it is self-betrayal since they deprive themselves of a future filled with people who trust them. And no one will allow them in.

Enlightened self-interest prevents you from doing many things in life that you could have enjoyed or benefited from, such as taunting and provoking your spouse to relieve boredom, having an affair and jeopardizing your marriage, stealing the candy bar, workplace fraud, telling pointless lies to gain esteem, and betraying your promises or loyalties for small gains. Many short-term benefits in life are foregone because you intuitively view them to be long-term losses.

The narcissist's myopia causes them to be unable to envisage the long run, giving them an insignificant picture of life, where short-term benefits lead to no long-term repercussions, and nothing prevents them from snatching that candy bar. This is due to their incapacity to empathize with their future self; therefore, they take from their future, essentially stealing from themselves.

Without the headwinds of morality or enlightened self-interest, the narcissist goes on a lifetime course to polish their lying, cheating, thieving, and backstabbing talents.

The narcissist sees the riches of all their ill-gotten earnings, which drives them to regard normal people as weak and foolish since they cannot achieve the things that come so readily to the narcissist and from which the narcissist derives so many advantages.

When we lie, cheat, steal, or backstab, we unconsciously make half-hearted efforts that reduce our chances of success and increase our chances of failure. Eventually, we learn from the pain of being caught that it's not worth it, and so we learn to prefer the honest path in life, simply because it is less painful for us.

The narcissist embraced the arts of lying, cheating, stealing, and backstabbing as an artist from the outset, totally devoted to seeing the undertaking through wholeheartedly. These arts have only given them benefits, not punishment, because, unlike us, they were generally effective for the narcissist.

It is both a shame and a thrill to them that you are unable to master these abilities. The narcissist is so effective at manipulation because they initially manipulated themselves.

They deceive themselves, take from their future, and violate all love until there is no love left, even self-love. They've twisted themselves into a corner inside, making them desperate to make manipulation work.

Manipulation is all they have left in life; it's the only technique they employ to cope with any life situation; they have unknowingly driven themselves to become highly adept at their sole tool since they have no other skills to get through life.

This makes them very simple to decipher. If you know how.

CHAPTER 5

Can you persuade a manipulator?

I don't believe you can ever successfully influence a manipulator. They're simply too brilliant at what they do. Remember, this is life or death for them, and this is all they know and have done their whole lives.

What you can do **is strengthen yourself!! st r.o.n.g.!** directly from the inside! stop focusing on the narcissist, whomever they may be. Stop treating everything people say, do, think, comment, purchase, and look at, as if it applies to you. I know it FEELS and LOOKS personal, but it is not.

It's just the only way a manipulator knows how to live. What you should do is educate yourself. Educate yourself on all you can about these ill people.

How they work. What type of people they are? That is significant. They will either be overt or covert, and their methods will be very different. Discover their defense techniques, such as gaslighting, projection, triangulation, and flying monkeys.

Then, once you've learned everything you can about them, construct a set of armor for yourself. Discover why you were drawn to this individual. Find out what it was about you that drew them in. You are most likely a caring and compassionate person. To an extent. You most likely have no limits and let anyone walk all over you.

Or you simply don't know how to say **No**. Perhaps you, like me, were raised in a household full of narcissists who prepared you to be the ideal narcissistic candidate. From an early age, you were taught that the only way someone could love you was if you surrendered your entire soul.

You guessed it. Wrong response!! The only way to receive TRUE love is to first love yourself!! Anyone who tells you it's selfish to love yourself first and that it's bad to prioritize your own needs over those of others has a hidden agenda. What good are you to anyone if you're a complete mess?

If you're not sure what your limits are, the short solution is to write down exactly what behaviors you will NOT allow from ANYONE! That includes strangers as well as family members.

Especially those in your family who claim they love you, especially those who "say" they love you but their "actions" don't match the words coming out of their mouths lately.

People seem to feel that individuals in our family should be given second, third, fourth, fifth, sixth, etc., opportunities after they have repeatedly treated us brutally and never apologized. Why is this the case?! I believe that family members should be held to a higher standard.

They should be the ones whose behavior everyone else should aim to emulate. Above all, family should ALWAYS treat us better than everyone else. They are the only people that love us **UNCONSTITUTIONALLY!!** And if you are receiving anything other than this, you must break all links with them for your health and sanity.

They are poisonous, and they will make your life a miserable hell before they are finished with you. I know because I've been there and had to do it. It took me years to realize what was going on all around me, all of which was coordinated by my very own biological mother.

I left after Christmas in 2013, and I had no idea how great life might be. I lost my whole family because they all believed her lies or. I don't care anymore. I am liberated.

So, learn more about personal limits and become the number one person in your own life. Make yourself an advocate. Be brave. It won't be easy at first, but the more you do it, the more you'll enjoy it and feel better.

Finally, try to be as boring as possible! Avoid being a drama queen. You should not quarrel with them. (They'll simply twist everything anyhow) Don't be sucked into one of these words' debates where all they truly want to do is annoy you with loads of words.

When they start accusing you of stuff, pay attention because they will betray themselves without even realizing it. It's extremely interesting! They are projection masters.

That is, they can't bear the thought of knowing how nasty they are, so they blame it all on you. So, the next time someone tells you how nasty, greedy, sadistic, and terrible you are, pay attention. They are speaking about themselves. Every single phrase is about them.

So, in a nutshell, be strong for yourself, learn to love yourself FIRST, be boring, don't play their games, set and stick to personal boundaries, and listen instead of taking what they say personally. They are not speaking about you; rather, they are speaking about themselves. And you should never go near a narcissist without your armor on.

How do you control a narcissist?

So, I'm guessing your purpose is to attack them. I don't encourage behaving in this manner since it will create more grief than anything else, but here we go:

You must maintain the highest level of physical attractiveness at all times. To make this work, you must be above average. Be sure of yourself. If they point out your arrogance, respond, "I'm not arrogant; I'm persuaded." Look at the numbers."

Never tell them you adore them as well. Be aloof, noncommittal, and flirtatious. Not blatantly flirting, but ignorant flirty, so that when they lose their cool over it, you can turn it around to make them appear insane.

Underhandedly point up their flaws. (For example, you would have a flawless face if your nose were different, your eyes weren't so far apart, your chin was stronger, your nose wasn't so near to your upper lip, and so on.

It doesn't have to be real, but a manipulator will obsess over this flaw and demand your acceptance. (I like how at ease you are with yourself and don't mind if you look like crap or have gained a few pounds. You own it! Then poke their back fat, which everyone has a little bit of.

They will despise you if you poke and squeeze it adoringly). Give them anxieties so they would want your praise.

Always be occupied. However, don't abandon plans after they've been made.

Throw a tantrum now and then for no apparent reason. Overreact completely and then be unrepentant about it since you don't know how to cope with your feelings for them because you've never cared enough about someone to panic out. This will make them feel unique and will entice them to want to dominate you.

Carry on with this train disaster until you're tired of it, then go no contact. They'll either urgently strive to gain your attention or they won't.

They prefer disease, though, and the behavior described above is a sick relationship based on insecurity and manipulation.

Understand that managing them into being worth a damn and a wonderful spouse is impossible. They'll never adore you since they lack the capacity.

CHAPTER 6

How To Deal With Emotional Manipulative People

One of the first things we'll discuss is that many individuals who want control really suffer from anxiety. If they were reared in a setting where they felt highly out of control as children, they will have anxiety as adults.

When you have felt out of control in your life or have not learned how to fill yourself full, you will want to control things as an adult, or you will want people or things outside of you to fill you up since you did not learn how to do so.

You will discover that you do not need to put someone else down in order to feel good about yourself, regardless of how much self-esteem you have, whether it is little or a lot.

Nine times out of ten, a narcissistic person is unaware that they were reared in dysfunction. I know many people who don't know what happened to them during their childhood that caused them to be the way they are, so people who aren't curious about why they are this way are people who can't self-reflect, people who tend to be manipulative, and people who are so far down the hole that either they don't see the dysfunction or they can't face the dysfunction.

So, a manipulator will not be conscious that they are manipulating; they will not be aware that they are attempting to dominate another person or control the environment.

So, if you enjoy power and dominating others, That indicates your ego is in charge, and your ego feels it is correct, knows everything, and cannot accept criticism That is why most manipulators have that attitude or character: they cannot handle criticism and simply want to be in charge and get what they want and how they want it. It's a childish mindset.

Because manipulators aim to obtain control, they will investigate you and learn about you to see what strategies they may use to convince you to give them what they want. A manipulator will use three things to determine which one works best for you.

Fear

Guilt

Shame

Remember that manipulation 2 involves more than just using the term "guilt." A manipulator is grooming you; therefore, there will be gas lighting and a lot of other things stated. There will be a lot of these small things spoken in order for you to feel dread, remorse, or sadness. shame.

So, if a manipulator wants to use your guilt against you, they will say things like, you've never been there for me, and I care about you when you need assistance, but you're never there for me. They constantly play the victim, and they always use terms that make you out to be a really awful person.

Everything is designed to make you feel horrible about yourself. This is most common in all relationships. So, although they are portraying themselves as the victim in order for you to feel horrible for them or guilty that they are truly suffering, they hook you with that because you have already been hooked.

Just to entice you and persuade you to do what they want. That is, you must say yes to whatever they say in order to do what they want you to do, even if you don't want to.

But you have no choice since you are stuck. So, when a manipulator or narcissist utilizes fear in their words to dominate you, this is a red flag.

They realize you are dependent on them, that you rely on having them in your life, and how essential the connection is to you. When this happens, you are unable to provide yourself with the things that you require.

That suggests you lack self-care and don't know how to appreciate yourself. Once this individual realizes how much space they occupy in your life, every other person will feel threatened. They believe you require their approval to accomplish things.

That is how it works. If you are afraid of losing this person or that they will have a different opinion of you, or if you are afraid that other people will perceive you in the same light, then you will try to blend into their game and give them complete power over your brains by utilizing fear, guilt, and shame.

After you give them their way, they will warn you that if you don't do what they want, they will do this or that just to scare you.

They threaten you more because they believe you need them so badly, and they bring up things you did in the past to make you feel horrible about yourself.

This is when the shame game enters the picture. They evoke memories of the past. Most of the time, they do this to test your reaction or to see whether you are upset about what they said.

Then they discuss your reactions. So, when you feel weak or nervous, that is when they will exploit and shame you. They will make you feel as if you are the problem, as if something is wrong with you. That's why this individual is telling you this, or it's just the truth.

How To Respond Without Reacting

We've all been in a position when someone knows precisely where your pain spots are and knows what to say to make you feel useless. We've all met individuals like this before, whether they're relatives, friends, or partners, and it's often difficult to respond to them, especially when they're so unpleasant.

You must learn how to manage this scenario because when we start from a negative place, when we drop to the level of the other person, when we become emotional and believe that what someone is saying is unjust, hurtful, or incorrect, nothing positive comes of it.

I'm not saying you shouldn't stand up for yourself in a healthy way, which includes not speaking negatively to that individual. So, when someone comes at you, whether it's a narcissist or a poisonous person, and says something absurd, how do you deal with these situations?

So, you are stating that when we become emotional, what you said wounded me, and it will continue to pain you. Because you are human, it will be painful for you. One of the most important things to grasp in this sort of circumstance is that the person who is saying something absolutely nasty or incorrect is doing it to be the button pusher. So, you must take a step back and identify when people exhibit specific behaviors.

That is why I talk so much about emotional abusers, since the strategies that an emotional abuser would employ are not always black and white.

If someone is gas lighting you and you don't know what it means or don't know who you're dealing with, if you are coming from an insecure, co-dependent position where you lack a genuine sense of self, you will anticipate taking on that person's projection.

You don't know how to hold onto yourself, and if you don't have the self-confidence and self-love inside yourself to recognize when someone is projecting onto you, you'll accept it and be mistreated.

That's why I constantly tell people to prioritize themselves. However, you must recognize that what someone does to you is a reflection of themselves and has nothing to do with you. They may say things that cut you at the knees because they want to get to you, but what they are actually doing is attempting to relieve some of their own strain.

So, when someone does something utterly uncalled for and absurd, that person is hurting on the inside, and this is something you must realize when dealing with these types of people. When you realize this, you can take a step back and not take it personally.

So, it doesn't mean it doesn't hurt; it just means it's a reflection of that person, their insecurities, their own wounds, and how they feel about themselves on the inside, because anyone who is happy and healthy with themselves and loves themselves won't think of hurting anyone.

They don't say things to get a rise out of someone, and they don't do things to pull someone down in order to make themselves feel better. That is really crucial to comprehend. That is their way of making themselves feel better since they have an emptiness, a wound, envy, and insecurity inside them at all times.

They are filled with negative energy and want to harm others in order to feel better about themselves. And, while it may sound nasty and twisted, that is how manipulative people spend their lives. So, how do you deal with people like this?

Number one is if you are not at a place inside yourself or with this person where you can truly be in front of them and have this discussion when they are saying these things, and you can't simply not let it impact you. You must understand when to end a conversation.

This is not you standing up for yourself; it is you knowing when to leave. It is really more difficult to do than to allow your emotions to take over and simply respond. When you know your surroundings, no matter what someone says to you, you can keep your cool and say it.

What do you think? It's time for me to go. That is self-empowerment and self-care, and I know it may appear to others as a sign of weakness, but trust me, it is not. It is far easier to walk away than it is to stay in that environment and become emotionally attached to someone because that is what that person desires.

They want to see how their actions have impacted you.

That is where they know they are winning; they feel powerful now because they have influenced you, especially if you are in a setting with someone and things are heating up. If you need to, hang up the phone or walk away; simply tell them you'll call them later or that you need to do something.

So, you just walk away, and then things are over. At the end of the conversation, it's just about arming yourself to say that I am not engaging in this behavior. If you can't respond, and if you know you don't have the willpower or energy to respond to this type of person, then you need to leave the situation that allows you to keep yourself intact and still not have to let the person affect you.

People may say you're leaving because you can't take it, and that's perfectly OK. They can say that as long as you are aware that you are withdrawing yourself. That is, you are not letting those feelings surface, whether they be tears or fury. You know, showing that individual that they have you or that they have won is all that you need to say to that person.

Hey! I'm sorry you feel that way, but I'm not going to be around someone who speaks to me in that manner, and that's all there is to it. Short and sweet. You then turn around and walk away. With this, even after you say it and go to your room to cry alone, not in front of them, you've won.

You just conveyed the idea that you love yourself and are terrific.

CHAPTER 7

What are the true colours of a narcissist?

Words used to denigrate are particularly noxious. A lack of empathy is evident, which may perplex you when they wish to love-bomb you.

Attempts towards isolation. Smearing family members on purpose so that I may see my family differently.

Personal Story From A Follower

I'm enraged over little matters. This was quite upsetting for me. Today, I can't bear hearing anyone yell. I simply vanish. You require assistance. A narcissist just turns away. I had a bad knee injury and had to care for two kids. He pretended to be deaf and still left me alone. Naturally, my knee swelled up more and more.

Treatment in complete silence. He would serve me silence if he didn't have a fast response to justify his behavior. Or maybe love bombing someone.

He was looking for a new place to live. When my first utility bill arrived, I assumed it was a real error on the part of the energy provider. My suspicions were raised the second time. Yes, he attempted to dupe me.

So, I'm working hard to pay for independent school tuition, while Mr. entitled is squandering it on his numerous excursions.

I had a sneaking suspicion that he was cheating. He was an expert at concealment. I attempted to find evidence of this but was unable. But I was aware that this was taking place.

Expectations are high. The moment he parks his car, that should instantly signal that the dish is ready to be served.

I'll be called a lot of names if I'm five minutes late for work.

The youngsters accomplish something. It's all his fault. The children are misbehaving. It's all my fault.

He calls me a horrible mother because I work, yet he enjoys spending what I make. Hypocrite!

Control - wants me to cease working yet unable to provide me with the funds to maintain my boys in an independent school. He wanted me to be financially reliant on him.

Please never rely on a narcissist for financial support. That will be your undoing.
When in the company of other girls, she tries to make me envious. I had ceased caring by the time I had my sons. You simply tire.

Refusing to participate in any family activities. I'm sure many assumed I was divorced a long time ago.
There is no self-control. This was terrifying. You notice that this individual is unable to manage his rage.

So many lies and deception. When you catch him, he weaves additional falsehoods while keeping a straight face.

Guilty pleasure. He criticizes me for not keeping the house immaculately and clean, yet he does nothing to help. But I also have two children, a house, and a job. Woman of strength!

Obligations. One small task he completes implies he has completed the Great Wall of China for you.

Lazy. Lots of nonsense rhetoric but accomplishing nothing. I believe they are afraid of the future because they are cowards at heart.

Bullying. There are far too many episodes.

He is ill. Everyone's life comes to a halt, and we are all slaves. I became ill. What does it matter?

Ugly memories, and thank God I was able to leave this dreadful marriage. If I had continued in these circumstances, there is no chance I would have avoided chronic disease or insanity.

CHAPTER 8

Why are manipulators interested in gaslighting you?

Manipulator get away with their malicious deeds by convincing you that what's true isn't, and what's not true is true, that's how they get away with whatever it is they want to get away with, it's an advanced form of 'I didn't do it,' or 'it wasn't me' that children do (e.g. they didn't have an affair, it was you)

Gaslighting is the ultimate in individuals because the entire point of gaslighting can be summarized as 'you're crazy (or stupid) because I disagree with everything you say or think no matter how reasonable you sound (or how much evidence you provide)'.

It's weaponized invalidation; by invalidating everything you own, you no longer know what to say or think, leaving you in a perpetual state of cognitive dissonance (very mentally unpleasant) and the narcissist in a perpetual state of delight.

Furthermore, every idea or conviction that the manipulator present as an alternative to yours is opposed to yours. They are so opposed that you cannot meet them halfway; you must either renounce truth (and sanity) and believe them or argue with them. It is no coincidence that they always arrive at the exact opposite of you and yours.

Their viewpoints will be opposed to yours. Their presents will be the polar opposite of what you requested. They will be too late to meet you at the airport. Contrarianism and passive aggressiveness collide in gaslighting.

The goal is to get a high by causing cognitive dissonance. Your annoyance is not an accident. As a result, they will do so even if there is no malicious deed to commit. It's entertainment for them.

You are governed by your views, and nothing has more power than controlling your beliefs about reality. You will be forced to quit your original route and travel in the direction the narcissist desires by convincing you of untrue unreality and disbelieving your honest views.

If you are subjected to this a thousand times, you will become programmed to immediately forsake your thoughts and answer every tug on the leash. Like a stupid animal, you will be led anywhere the narcissists desire (and the direction will continually vary whimsically since you are being covertly led nowhere).

This is how your soul and will are shattered. This is how you are forcibly transformed from a human to a beast of burden or an appliance.

What is the single point that connects all three points?

Narcissists like playing with you. Toying with you gives vital entertainment, makes life meaningful, and helps them to get through the day, without which they would become bored, and boredom feels like suicidal sadness to a narcissist (boredom is far worse for them than for you). That's why they have to play with you for their good.

So, you need to understand the motivation behind gaslighting (playing with you to cause cognitive dissonance for fun) and the methods (being contrarian, being pointlessly oppositional, invalidation, deliberate misunderstanding, and misinterpretation) so you know this is just a game they don't take seriously, which means you need to keep second-guessing them and remind yourself never to be earnest with them.

Gaslighting Is Also A Type of Psychic Assault.

We expect a real reflection when we express ourselves. It's gratifying when it happens. It has nothing to do with whether people agree or disagree with our points of view, or whether they praise or criticize us.

As long as the reflection is real, it is beneficial and nurturing since it is sensible and reasonable, which includes telling us "No" or exposing our defects. Other individuals serve as mirrors for us, and we learn about ourselves by looking in the mirror.

What we see is who we are as long as the mirror is rational and reasonable, and the image is true. Knowing who we are helps us navigate through life.

The manipulator ensures that a funhouse mirror returns a distorted reflection so that you only 'know' a diseased, false version of yourself (and hopefully one day believe you are sick and twisted and get ill as well).

Once again, it is the unreasonableness of the reflection that is detrimental, not the 'yes' or 'no', praise, or condemnation. When we are confronted with a warped mirror, it not only invalidates us but also tampers with our sanity and affects our psychic health. It damages our spirit and causes us to take wrong turns in life. This is intentional.

For example, the narcissist violates your soul by misinterpreting everything you say, returning answers that have nothing to do with the question, pretending not to hear you, answering 'no' precisely because the only reasonable response is 'yes,' or answering 'I don't know' when they know you suspect they do know.

The manipulators self is the assertion that we are ill and twisted, that we can't say anything correctly, and that we can't receive any accurate replies from him. The narcissist's reactions will only reveal lunacy about ourselves.

That is what gaslighting's psychic assault is all about. Psychic punching you.

At the very least, purposeful criticisms break you down. You get a frontal punch. That is painful, but the front is sturdy and resilient. But pretending you said something else, heard something different, didn't say anything, or that you heard them when you didn't is like getting punched from behind, above, below, or either side.

Most importantly, you naturally perceive deliberate criticisms as a punch (a form of aggression), so you harden up and become avoidant, but you don't naturally perceive gaslighting as a punch, so you open up to try harder and clarify with the narcissist, you've just fallen into their trap, and even more gaslighting will follow.

The entire day is consumed with attempting to answer the first inquiry. As a result, gaslighting penetrates more quickly and profoundly than purposeful criticism.

Another example: you ask what's for dinner, and the narcissist replies, 'You mean lunch? supper will be ready in 5 minutes instead. You are frustrated. But the irritation comes from the answer's utter disrespect, not from not getting your way. That was done on purpose. The narcissist pummels us with their psychological fist each time, hopefully into wrath or insanity.

You still don't know what's for dinner, you weren't referring to lunch, you didn't want to know when dinner will be ready, you just wanted someone to acknowledge your existence through your question,

But instead, you got someone who pretended you asked a different question and gave you irrelevant information just to covertly mess with you to make you feel non-existent by ensuring you never get your answer (but you get a lot of everything else that you never wanted). The whole aim was to annoy you while concealing it.

You'll go insane if every question you ask is met with a humorous response, everything you say is disregarded or replied with purposeful unreasonableness, you get favors you never asked for, and you never get anything you truly asked for, and this continues for years. That's the strategy.

Narcissist hopes you never learn these secrets.

What they genuinely are on the inside: empty, shattered, fractured, agitated, restless, nervous, dissatisfied, jealous, poor self-esteem, unstable identity, and what terrible ideas they have hidden within themselves from infancy.

That the narcissist badly needs you to validate them. They must control their emotions and maintain a healthy sense of self. I heard an expert in the region say today, "Picture a cup with a hole in the bottom," alluding to an NPD person's incessant need for confirmation or validation.

Their persistent low self-esteem, negative self-talk, and poor self-image. They do not want you to know. Getting your initial reaction begins the imbalance, their leverage.

A small jab, ridicule, poke, or tease you about height, weight, ethnicity, religion, poor, rich, hair, age, or clothing - devaluation, humiliation, bullying, cruel, offers to hook you, trap you, beat you, dominate you, entice you, trick you, win, control you, even in the most subtle of ways, anything to destabilize and control you. When a newbie enters a social circle, the narcissist is the one who needs to say something rude, cutesy, or a backhanded compliment about the newcomer. Possession of power. Overt flattery is another narc trait.

My aunt has made strange phone calls just asking questions like "Who is the most important person in your life?" and "What moves you?" All of them were probing and looking for soft areas. I reframed it so she could get to know me better. Ha.

Manipulators desire to be viewed as powerful, important, and significant. They have none of these characteristics below. Manipulators are nervous with individuals who are confident, self-loving, honest, cheerful, powerful, and direct; the narcissist has no power, no comprehension of these people, no way to build traps, no way to hook.

Attempts at charm, enticement, and manipulation by narcissists fail. Narcissists use defective neural circuitry, a damaged region of the brain caused by a traumatic childhood that resulted in an abnormal psychological disorder.

Understand where it came from very genuine emotions that resulted in very real brain chemistry throughout brain development. They have been frozen in time as a mistreated child, and they are now that infant in an adult body, wanting care and calm from a neurotypical loving mother they have never known.

Because their mother did not teach them love, they do not understand the language or frequency of love. Beware and take note, whatever adult affection or pity you have is misplaced, the infant is gone, and you are now dealing with an angry predator.

The narcissist will demonstrate their lack of concern for others through gossip, broken relationships, hierarchical thinking, hypocritical behavior, no touch with their family of origin, mental/verbal abuse, violence/murder, and they don't care about you as a person, only as a source of supply.

People currently play ridiculous games on Quora and other media, making allegations using the word "narcissist." To attain a goal here or there, 99% of us may utilize or practice a narcissistic tendency. Any pattern of qualities, in my opinion, tips the needle into a condition at this point. Does it make sense? it is when the support of the idealized self/false image becomes the primary objective, a means unto itself.

In other words, many of us use bravado, pick-up artistry, circus barking, salesmanship, ego, omission, lying, and fibbing, the fish was THIS huge, and we do it with an underlying purpose in mind. To succeed, make money, stand out, get the lady, or anything else. A narcissist will do anything for the sake of the image, and just the image.

This is why you witness rageful outbursts when criticizing or pointing out anything that contradicts any of the nonsense they broadcast. The ego's frailty.

A narcissist is NOTHING without his or her image. If your spouse, wife, boyfriend, or girlfriend cheated, shouted, or lied, it does not make them a narcissist.

Make no misconceptions or misunderstandings about a truly disturbed narcissist; you are in grave danger in their presence. They are the sort who, if given the chance, would shove their child down a cliff if it served their image. If you are conscious, the narcissistic pattern of behavior ALWAYS exposes itself.

The narcissist does not want you to know that they lack a moral compass and an inherent value system that produces honest, dependable, predictable, and principled behavior. Whatever they do, follow, or value must have only one purpose: to strengthen their fake self, idealized image.

This is why narcissists are found acting differently in different situations. "Playing to the room" is an act in which they keep their social groupings apart from one another. Manipulators can range from brilliant doctors to destitute drug addicts, and they might be very clever or have low IQs. Honesty or deception? Can even be truthful about many things if it helps them view themselves better. Narcissists are as straightforward as that.

Their patterns of abuse, triggers, and manipulation may appear intricate or tiring, and they are, but the machine calling the shots is extremely simple in its requirements.

The narcissist does not want you to learn that you have desirable qualities such as authenticity, creating, building, acceptance by others, social skills, beauty, money, accomplishments, friends, giving love, being loved, empathy, and strength, and they see you as better than themselves. They admire you and aspire to be like you.

Narcissists hope you never find out that they have sex with your wife, spouse, family member, married neighbor, or anybody else who has an impact on you. Narcissists seek to destabilize you by taking your friends, children, spouse, or anybody else. They are dissatisfied and want you to "experience their anguish."

That they have previously been rejected for the same reason you will shortly be rejecting them. You got them again. They must keep the ugly envious abusive beast inside them hidden. It is tiring for them to always be in conflict, maintain a fake ego, and employ mental acrobatics to avoid accountability.

You can see the exhaustion taking its toll on their eyes, causing them to age faster than expected. True story: diagnosed with NPD, I've known him for 18 years, 6'5 collegiate quarterback on a national championship football team, and undoubtedly one of the finest looking guys in the United States at the age of 23.

Narcissists do not want you to know about all the human devastation, grief, divorces, cruelty, pointless verbal abuse, malicious falsehoods, shattered relationships, and actual hurt they have caused in the past. Internet dating allows narcissists to spread their cruelty around the globe anonymously and without responsibility.

How much they despise themselves and the uncontrollable wrath, unbearable anguish, insatiable predatory tendencies to get supply, the addictions they have to comfort themselves, the emptiness, feelings of unworthiness, and poor self-esteem they carry around with them daily.

Narcissists don't want you to know how much they admire you. They want your happiness, your childhood, your spouse, your mind, your business, your friends, your teeth, your energy, your experience, your clothes, your money, your parents, your neighborhood, your children, your parenting abilities, your style, your name, your smell, your house; they want to be you.

You are their fresh beginning. Narcissists are mental cannibals, consuming others to escape from what is inside themselves. Many narcissists work as "luxury high-end" real estate agents, flocking towards wealthy people, flattering wealthy people,

Seeking any position around ultra-wealthy people, all to enhance their image of wealth, knowing powerful people, name-dropping, having the right connections, power, and significance.

Our young are encouraged, promoted, and created with this image-based phony life mentality by social media. Bravo TV has earned a lot of money off of underpaid narcissists doing their stunts. All you have to do is switch on the cameras and watch the drama and illusion.

Narcissists hope you never discover that their suicide threats are total fabrications and desperate pleas for attention. "Well, no one wants me, so I guess it's best if I simply don't come here," "I've been thinking about killing myself," everything to attract attention, all to escape whatever crime, theft, following a breakup, abuse to a person they are involved in. Look over here at this hand, not at the shambles I've produced over there. A distraction, a change of focus.

Narcissists will do this to cancer-stricken elderly family members who require their aid. The narcissist is now straining an already sick individual and diverting family attention away from another's actual medical needs.

Narcissists don't want you to realize that invitations, offers, phone calls, and presents might all have a hidden reason or contribute to a running tally of what you owe them. Collect data on you, ask you questions about your money, house, marriage, prior failures, and past abuse, all while looking for flaws and hoping for a failure in your life that they can exploit or bad data to use against you in the future.

During a phone contact, look for the narc pattern, which will be a checklist of questions about your career, money, sickness, and family, similar to taking inventory of information they may then distort and gossip about you to others or take advantage of every chance you provide.

Narcissists will get to know someone else via you and give you something in exchange for something in the future. Narcissists have a hidden motivation, a trap for you, and a hidden plan. Betrayal and abuse provide a tremendous emotion that converts desire into a narcotic.

Have you ever seen a homeless man holding a sign saying he only wants to feed his family and children? They are not full-disclosure people; they are not upfront; there is always something else going on, and they purposefully impede your entire knowledge. When they finish talking, look for the scary gaze to check whether their charm is working.

Narcissists do not want you to discover that they are poor parents. Neurotypical women have an innate command, a biological imperative, a touch, a feel, a sound, real love, and an everlasting untiring commitment to the child they have made.

Always putting the needs of the kid first. Narcissists have no empathy; they can't even place their infants in front of themselves. Narcissists are backward and lack these skills. Children are expected to serve their mothers.

My birth mother uttered these identical words to me when I was 35 after I was placed for adoption on the first day of my life. "If you hadn't been born, I would have had a lovely husband and three children, two of whom would be looking after me right now." I inherited money and was married twice after my birth.

A full fantasy existence that should have happened except for me as a newborn baby. It's entirely my fault. Truly insane, and the danger to me or you are extremely serious.

Narcissists don't want you to know that they are walking black holes. They are continuously sucking into them, narcissists are destroyers, not creators. They always send forth bad energy and hurt someone.

With a narcissist, there is no equal sharing symbiotic partnership; it is parasitic or spiderlike by purpose. Narcissists can have high or low IQs, and they can work hard in certain situations, but their successes all serve to elevate themselves.

Narcissists do not want you to realize that they lack basic sympathetic communication abilities. Instigating conversations that begin with you on the defensive. A discussion in which they begin with an allegation or something they "heard" about you, a talk with a concealed agenda, or a conversation in which they begin with a question to which they already know the answer.

"Do you enjoy where you live?" was a recent conversation I was dragged into, which quickly devolved into my narcissistic aunt indicating that if she moved in with me, I would be under her control.

They are just interested in what they can obtain from you. Narcissists talk at you, attempting to program you with what they want you to believe and how they want you to view them, delusions, falsehoods, and exaggerations about themselves, your thoughts or opinions matter nothing to them, and they want you to be a flexible receptacle and swallow the verbal garbage they spew.

If you have anything to say, they may listen but have no guidance or concern. They may blab on and on about their beauty, who is rich, other people's money, they are related to a king, home value, their spouse's success, how much something is worth, hierarchical patterns, males seem to state numbers, "I'm worth a million," and so on for 20+ minutes without your participation in the conversation. Exhausting.

Narcissists don't want you to grasp how their schemes function. On-off, nice-nasty, punishment-reward, abuse-amends, enticements-let downs, future fake-withdrawal, gifts-you owe them, invitations-expectations, hot-cold, screaming-apologies, public humiliation-prayers for pardon, promises of reform.

Yesterday did not occur as you recall, tomorrow will be rainbows and puppies, and today you will confirm their fake self. Always chiseling away at your organization. Narcissistic abuse has an impact on our limbic system, which is a very basic area of our brain.

This maltreatment is felt in your gut. Train yourself to respond to the "ill" feeling, take action, and trust yourself. When confronted with such abuse, forget being nice.

Narcissists prefer that you not realize they have no friends or family. Slaves and captives are held by narcissists.

Narcissists do not want you to realize how bored and uninteresting they genuinely are. They may be flamboyant, carry a parrot on their shoulder as a prop, use animals to attract attention, wear attention-grabbing apparel, 40 cats, headgear, jewelry, obtain a nice automobile, and tell dramatic stories, for example.

They served in the special forces, attended Harvard, and knew a renowned person. Behind that vibrant façade lies an extremely dull and uninteresting individual. Liars and con artists. Behind those big stories and theatrics lies a coward, bully, unhappy, cheater, and bitter loser.

Narcissists do not want you to know that they no longer believe in their worth, hard work, virtue, kindness, merit, and devotion to others. This is precisely why you witness their predatory behaviors; they are unable to produce and must therefore take, resulting in desperation in their later years.

That superiority complex is an inferiority complex. Narcissists are effectively in a hole; you want to assist, and you've attempted to throw them a rope, but you're thinking from a neurotypical perspective. The situation is emptier of logic and common sense than you may realize.

You're effectively tying a noose around an infant's neck. The narcissistic newborn brain is at a loss about what to do with the rope. "Hey, quit trying to injure me with that rope! It smacked me in the head!" exclaimed the infant.

This stems from their initial narcissistic harm as an infant. Understand that their debut to the world was not filled with warm, loving motherly love. Their perspective on relationships and love is twisted as a result of their first relationship, a flaw if you will.

They cannot care about you because they lack the neurological circuitry required for empathy. When they emerge into neurotypical reality, they will have to look back at the hole they have been in their entire existence and realize the casualties they have caused. And what better location than a dark pit to project their vivid fantasies of a life they'd rather be living?

The greatest technique for spotting disturbed folks is to just observe, listen, and pay attention to what a person does over time rather than what they say. If they are a true narcissist, there will always be a pattern, repeating manipulations, poor empathy, wanton greed, and patterns of a skewed perspective of reality will develop.

After reading this, you may see some new possibilities in your life. Social media and reality are making a selfish image-based existence acceptable and even a full-time profession. "I'm an influencer" Fake life based on images fills reality programs, makes individuals famous, and may be beneficial for a few whiles damaging many more lives.

This has never happened before in the history of our species. This, in my opinion, is creating a genuine devolution of the whole human species in a path that is not beneficial to society as a whole. Look around you, homeless folks; they all appear to have a smartphone in the United States.

I just apprehended the arsonist who set fire to a property I own, costing over a million dollars in damage. I checked his social media and discovered that he is preaching about God and soliciting funds for a disabled woman's GoFundMe account.

With likes and upvotes, his pals are rooting for him. Social media consumes millions of people's whole days, creating a fictitious existence within a phone.
The sci-fi book forecast of the 1984 novel Neuromancer has arrived.

Your greatest tools for narco-proofing your life.

Be busy, serve others, work, have real-world skill or skills, be as independent as possible, give to others without expectation, do not lean into relationships, do not use other people to an abusive extent, be careful with what you reveal to others, listen to yourself speak, avoid gossip,

Take a true inventory of your effects on others, and avoid speaking about yourself as a victim, narcissists are wolves who seek vulnerabilities in others. Do not be concerned with diagnoses or labels; instead, investigate narcissistic patterns of behavior and abuse. People should not be labeled as narcissists or empaths. When you detect a narcissistic pattern of abuse directed against you, simply depart discreetly. Be true to yourself and love yourself.

Secret no. 2

They don't want you to know the truth about who they truly are and what they truly desire from you. In a nutshell, that's it. I'll use an example to make my argument. Do you believe you'd want to get to know someone better or dedicate time, energy, or resources to a relationship if they said the following to you?

"Hello, I'm interested in you because you're compassionate, kind, loving, and generous." I believe you would meet all of my needs, at least in the near term. I believe I could shape you into the person I want you to be because I am uninterested in who you truly are."

"Our "contract" will function well as long as you agree to all of my ideas and goals, as long as you listen to everything and prefer just one-sided interactions." I pretend to be a great kind person, but I have no goodness in me...it's all about me, me, and me.

My favorite topic to discuss is...me. I'm a complete gossip, hypocritical, vindictive, bossy, controlling, incredibly manipulative, a compulsive liar, terribly insecure, and self-loathing. All of those negative personality qualities are the result of never developing above the age of a three or four-year-old."

Because I'm emotionally stunted, I'll never be able to accept responsibility for anything...I'm an infant covered in adult skin (and I'm aware of it). I think in a really strange way. I'll never love you or have any kind of closeness with you because, well, I can't offer you what I don't have. I've never received the affection I needed to grow into a healthy child and an adult.

Instead, all I can do is pretend to offer you what I believe looks like it...at least for a little while. At my finest, I have an Oscar-worthy performance. Due to my immature lack of emotional intelligence, I have no idea how to be in a good mutually loving relationship.

I don't change because I don't believe I need to alter anything about myself.

I'm bound to keep repeating my version of insanity through established thinking and behavioral patterns that produce the same unpleasant and troublesome outcomes...more destruction and shattered relationships."

"I'd love to entangle you in my web of deception so I may take as much as I can from you without offering anything in return." I'll think about it a lot and occasionally hint at it to keep you off-balance and provoke a reaction from you.

I truly believe you are foolish in comparison to me, and I will remind you of this frequently...both overtly and covertly."

"I'll never tell you the truth." I may tell you half-truths, but you'll never receive the whole truth. I just believe my falsehoods. Of course, I'll be talking about myself the entire time. Did I mention how much I enjoy discussing myself and my life? If you don't continually admire and pay attention to me, I'll cut you off and talk over you...about me.

I may just withhold affection, sex, or anything else I know you desire to punish me for not doing what I want you to do. I'm going to make backup plans in case you don't give me what I want or I become bored because it's your fault.

Don't forget about it. It is your fault, not mine. Never my fault. When you view anything as "wrong," everything I do is your fault. Because I don't do anything wrong, it's all your responsibility. Period."

"I'll confuse you with word salad." I am frightened of rejection; therefore, your life will no longer be your own because I must control everything, and I mean everything. That covers everything about you, what you do, who you hang out with, what you think...everything.

I'll influence you in ways you never believed possible, and I'll do anything and everything I can to utterly master you. This makes me feel a lot better about myself, so I do it. So why are we fighting it? Everything will be fine...for me if you just give me what I want when I want it. You will not have any rights here.

You will be mine. It's pointless to object or oppose it. You'll lose the debate because you're not as intelligent as I am. Have I already told you that I believe you're stupid? So, I believe you are foolish. Just follow me and don't make any noise. Simply do not."

"On the inside, I'm empty. I'd like to call it a void, but it's more akin to the abyss and an endless pit of darkness and emptiness. I'm insecure and feel completely inadequate in every way.

That is why I want to utilize you as much and as frequently as possible. You have absolutely no say in the issue. What you believe and feel signifies nothing, zilch, nada, nights...nothing. You'll never know since I'll look to be the "hero" with my mask on. I'll be more than "special," superior to everyone, including you...I'll come out as confident and accomplished. I'll reflect on you. "I'm confident you'll enjoy my performance."

"I just want you to know that I'll never be the love of your life (despite my best efforts), but I will subject you to a gradual, subtle kind of misery on earth akin to Chinese torture." It will ultimately degrade you physically and psychologically, and I will love seeing you squirm and bewildered because it only demonstrates that I am better than you. I might even give you "the smirk" now and again.

I will never, ever love you! In that case, I won't like you. I will not respect you and will grow to despise you as time passes because I just do not care. My disgust for you will only increase."

"I know you'll buy my sales pitch because you can't help yourself and because I've had so many years to polish it (and you're simply too stupid to figure out my scam)." I did say I'm an Oscar-worthy performer, didn't I? So, after all of that, what do you think?

Do you want to give it a shot? I believe we have a chance. I've never met someone quite like you. I just know you're my soulmate. I've never loved somebody as much as I love you. You're just incredible.

I'm obsessed with you and can't get enough of you. I don't think I'd be able to live without you. "I adore you from the bottom of my heart."

So, what do you suppose they're hiding?

About Margie J. Larue

Margie J. Larue is a passionate relationship coach, devoted wife, and loving mother of three beautiful children. With a heart full of empathy and a desire to see people thrive in their relationships, Margie has dedicated her life to helping couples and individuals build strong, fulfilling connections.

Professional Journey

Margie's journey into relationship coaching began with her own experiences and challenges in love and family life. As a young adult, she faced her fair share of relationship ups and downs, but instead of allowing these obstacles to define her, she turned them into opportunities for growth and learning.

Combining her natural gift of understanding people's emotions with her academic background in psychology, Margie pursued a career as a certified relationship coach. She completed her studies at a renowned institution, honing her skills in communication, conflict resolution, and the intricacies of human connections.

Passion for Empowering Relationships

Margie's passion for helping others find love, happiness, and fulfillment in their relationships is evident in every aspect of her work. As a coach, she adopts a personalized and holistic approach, recognizing that every individual and relationship is unique. Her warm and non-judgmental demeanor creates a safe space for her clients to open up, fostering an environment of trust and vulnerability.

Through one-on-one coaching sessions and workshops, Margie equips her clients with valuable tools and techniques to improve their communication, strengthen their emotional bonds, and overcome challenges together. She firmly believes that healthy relationships are built on a foundation of understanding, respect, and effective communication.

Balancing Motherhood and Career

As a mother of three, Margie understands the importance of maintaining a healthy work-life balance. She cherishes her role as a mother and acknowledges that her experiences in parenting have enriched her insights as a relationship coach.

Her ability to empathize and relate to the challenges faced by couples and families is a testament to her dedication and authenticity. Outside of her professional pursuits, Margie enjoys spending quality time with her family, whether it's exploring nature, embarking on fun adventures, or simply enjoying cozy movie nights together.

Inspiring Change, One Relationship at a Time

Margie J. Larue's mission is to inspire positive change in relationships, empowering individuals and couples to create lasting, loving bonds. Her commitment to helping people navigate the complexities of love and family life has touched the lives of many, leaving behind a trail of transformed relationships and happy hearts.

If you're seeking guidance and support to strengthen your relationship or navigate through tough times, Margie J. Larue is the empathetic and skilled coach you can trust to walk with you on this transformative journey. Reach out to her today and embark on a path toward a more fulfilling and connected life with your loved ones.